What in the World is God Up To?

Why things are the way they are and why you should believe.

Other books by Andy Van Loenen...
Justice for Amy
Missing and Presumed Dead

What in the World is God Up To?

Why things are the way they are and why you should believe.

Andy Van Loenen

 Iroquois Point Publishing
Grand Rapids, Michigan

What in the World is God up To?
Why things are the way they are and why you should believe.
Copyright © 2015 Andrew E. Van Loenen III

Unless otherwise indicated, Scripture quotations are taken from the *New American Standard Bible,* NASB, Copyright © 1960, 1962, 1963, 1968, 1971, 1972, 1973, 1975, 1977 by the Lockman Foundation. Used by permission.

Citations marked "literal," taken from *The Interlinear Greek-English New Testament*, Copyright © 1980, 1981, 1983, 1984 by Jay P. Green Sr. Published by Hendrickson Publishers.

Published by Iroquois Point Publishing
Grand Rapids, Michigan USA

Printed in the United States of America

ISBN: 978-0-9835759-3-1

This book is a revised and updated version of the author's previous work, *What in the World is God Up To?: Why things are the way they are and what you can do about it.* It replaces that volume.

Contents

*For my Dad, who laid hold of the promise
and now beholds the face of God.*

Laying a Foundation

1

Laying a Foundation

W hen you write a book with a provocative title like this one, there is no way to know who will pick it up and read it. For that reason, I think it is important for you to know at the outset: What I'm basing my ideas on, by what logical process I formed these ideas, and what I'm asking you to believe as a foundation for the points that I'll make in this book. As a reader, you are entitled to know these things. As an author, my desire is to be as honest with you as I can.

From the title you've already guessed that this is a book about what God was and is up to. But why write such a book? The answer, in a word, is *perspective*. Most thinking people know that things are not right in this world. Sickness, suffering, fear, crime, poverty, graft, nations in turmoil, political corruption, and a host of other evils still exist, and in many cases are getting worse, in our highly educated and enlightened age. These things affect all of us and some of us more than others. My goal is to offer a perspective on how things got to be the way they are, what the implications are for us as human beings, and what we can do for ourselves and others in light of those things.

As an author, this is a book I have wanted to write for some time. However, it seemed to me that it would be the height of arrogance to attempt to tell others what God is up to. But, as a longtime student of theology, I was struck one day with a realization: if you read Augustine, John Calvin, L.S. Chafer, Norman Geisler, or any of the many others who have propounded theological ideas in books, unless they are exactly quoting God's words, you are reading their opinions. They may be well-supported opinions backed up with copious footnotes (other people's opinions), but they are opinions nonetheless. This is not to say that their opinions are wrong or of no value. Just that you don't usually realize that you're reading the opinions of others.

I want you to understand, up front, that unless I am exactly quoting God's Word, what you are reading are the ideas and opinions of a fallible man, offered in humility.

Gaining a Background Understanding

In the spiritual realm there is no greater question than that of authority. What a person believes is based solely on whatever authority or authorities that person accepts as the basis for those beliefs.

In order to adequately address the issue of authority from a logical perspective, it is necessary to begin at the beginning. For those of us who claim a belief in God, that beginning is the creation of the world.

It is also necessary to make some assumptions. However, the assumptions made here are those that I think a reasonable person could make:

> ➢ The world did not create itself. Therefore,
> ➢ There must have been a creator, and
> ➢ That creator is the One we call God.

From a logical perspective, if God created the world He could not *be* the world or any part of the world, as this would require Him to create Himself. Imagine a cake, for example: The cake could not make itself and, if you made it, you are not the cake. Neither are you the flour, eggs, sugar, etc. that make up the cake. You have your existence completely apart from the cake. In like manner, God is apart from His creation. We, as created beings, require the creation (air, food, water, etc.) in order to exist. God has no such requirements; His existence is not enhanced by the creation, nor would it be diminished if the creation did not exist.

From man's perspective, the main ramification of God existing apart from His creation is that the creation has no *natural* way of knowing anything about God. This is true because His existence apart from the creation is, of necessity, apart from the sphere of the creation's ability to know. Consequently, the only way that the creation could know God or anything about God would be if He chose to reveal Himself to the creation. This He has done, and it is manifested primarily in two ways:

1. General revelation
2. Special revelation

General revelation includes the created order and the physical laws (for example, the law of gravity) that govern it. When man contemplates the creation, he sees order and, hopefully, intelligent design. Moreover, the deeper man looks into the creation, the more evidence he sees of intelligent design.

To cite an example: The human heart is an electrically operated pump. The electrical activity of the heart is such that the heart's natural pacemaker (the sinoatrial node) fires an electrical pulse toward the atrioventricular node. This pulse causes the heart's atria (the upper chambers) to contract, pumping blood from them into the ventricles (the lower chambers). When the pulse arrives at the atrioventricular node, it delays there for approximately 110 thousandths of a second to allow the ventricles to fill with blood before continuing on from the atrioventricular node to contract the ventricles, causing them to pump blood out to the body. This delay is relatively constant regardless of heart rate.[1]

The odds against the chance occurrence of the 110-millisecond delay at the atrioventricular node are so astronomical as to be absurd. Yet the heart could not properly function and we could not live without it. This argues strongly for intelligent creation.

To cite another example: DNA contains the genetic information code that is crucial to all living matter. While the chemical makeup of DNA is identical in every organism, a man is not a cabbage and a cabbage is not a cat. This is because the base *sequence* of DNA is different from organism to organism. In other words, the difference is in the way in which the DNA delivers *information*. This difference is coded in the DNA's molecular structure.

The presence of information and its communication *always* indicate the presence of intelligence. As a note of interest, the genetic information in each cell of the human body is equivalent to the information contained in a library of roughly 4,000 books.

But here's the rub: DNA cannot exist without the presence of at least 20 different types of proteins. However, these proteins can only be produced at the direction of the DNA. In other words, they had to come into existence simultaneously. This is a powerful argument because there is no way for this to occur apart from intelligent creation.[2]

Also part of God's general revelation is "natural law." Without going too deeply into it, the natural law is "written" on everyone's heart. This is how we innately know when what we or others are doing is wrong. Nobody needs to tell us; we just know.

Some have put this down to cultural mores, but this does not explain the universal sense of justice inherent in all people. For example: child abuse, murder, and stealing are considered to be wrong acts regardless of the culture in which one lives.

General revelation is important in that it leads one to believe that there is a higher being (God), leads one to generally obey the natural law, and to feel guilt when we don't. However, it does not really tell us anything specific *about* that God.

Special revelation is God actually telling us about Himself—who He is, what He is like, what He, as our Creator, Lord, and Judge expects of us, etc. This He has done primarily through His prophets and through His Son,

Jesus Christ. These things have been recorded for us in the Bible.

The Bible claims to be the very word of God. For example:

All Scripture is inspired by God [literally, God breathed] and profitable for teaching, for reproof, for correction, for training in righteousness; (2 Timothy 3:16)

But know this first of all, that no prophecy of Scripture is a matter of one's own interpretation, for no prophecy was ever made by an act of human will, but men moved by the Holy Spirit spoke from God. (2 Peter 1:20-21)

Jesus said of the Father's (God's) Word that it is truth:

Sanctify them in the truth; Thy word is truth. (John 17:17)

Moreover, God has said of Himself that He does not change (is immutable):

"For I, the Lord, do not change..." (Malachi 3:6)

Conclusive proof of the truthfulness of these statements is fulfilled prophecy. Every prophecy in the Bible with an intended historical fulfillment has been fulfilled to the letter. Did you know that there were hundreds of specific prophecies in the Old Testament related to the coming of the Messiah, all of them made hundreds of years before the Messiah (Christ) came, and all of them fulfilled precisely in Jesus Christ? Here are just a few examples:

That Christ would be born of a virgin
Old Testament Prophecy   *New Testament Fulfillment*
Isaiah 7:14   Matthew 1:23

That He would live in Nazareth of Galilee
Old Testament Prophecy   *New Testament Fulfillment*
Isaiah 9:1-2   Matthew 2:23, 4:15

That He would do miracles
Old Testament Prophecy   *New Testament Fulfillment*

7

| Isaiah 35:2-6, 61:1-2 | Matthew 9:35, Luke 4:16-21 |

That He would be betrayed by a friend for 30 pieces of silver

| *Old Testament Prophecy* | *New Testament Fulfillment* |
| Zechariah 11:12-13 | Matthew 27:9-10 |

That His hands and feet would be pierced

| *Old Testament Prophecy* | *New Testament Fulfillment* |
| Psalm 22:16 | Luke 23:33 |

That He would be crucified among thieves

| *Old Testament Prophecy* | *New Testament Fulfillment* |
| Isaiah 53:12 | Matthew 27:38 |

That His side would be pierced

| *Old Testament Prophecy* | *New Testament Fulfillment* |
| Zechariah 12:10 | John 19:34 |

That He would be buried in a rich man's tomb

| *Old Testament Prophecy* | *New Testament Fulfillment* |
| Isaiah 53:9 | Matthew 27:57-60 |

That He would rise from the dead

| *Old Testament Prophecy* | *New Testament Fulfillment* |
| Psalm 16:10 | Mark 16:6, Acts 2:31 |

That He would ascend into heaven

| *Old Testament Prophecy* | *New Testament Fulfillment* |
| Psalm 68:18 | Acts 1:9 |

Fulfilled prophecy is extremely important because God has given us a means of checking Him out. The graciousness of this is practically beyond comprehension. Given His existence outside of His creation and our inability to know Him by natural means, we would have no choice but to believe everything He told us—and that would have to be sufficient. However, He has allowed us to apply the test of fulfilled prophecy to understand with absolute certainty that His word is true.

This leads to three conclusions:

1. The Bible is God's Word.
2. God's Word is truth.

3. The truth presented in God's Word is unchanging.

The final point above is based on God's immutability (unchangeableness). In other words, if God does not change, what He has said was true at any point in time has always been true and always will be true.

These three points form the foundation from which I will proceed.

---

1. Joseph J. Carr and John M. Brown, *Introduction to Biomedical Equipment Technology* (John Wiley & Sons, 1981) pp. 17-18

2. Walter T. Brown Jr., *In the Beginning* (Center for Scientific Creation, 1986) p.6

In the Beginning

2

In the Beginning

T he Bible opens in Genesis 1:1 with, "In the beginning God created the heavens and the earth." From there it goes on to describe the creative activities of the six individual days in which God accomplished the creation.

My purpose is not to get into a discussion about the activities of each of those days, but to focus instead on the facts surrounding the sixth day; the day in which God created man:

Then God said, "Let Us make man in Our image, according to Our likeness; and let them rule over the fish of the sea and over the birds of the sky and over the cattle and over all the earth, and over every creeping thing that creeps on the earth." And God created man in His own image, in the image of God He created him; male and female He created them. (Genesis 1:26-27)

There are several things to be derived from these verses. First and somewhat tangential to our subject we read, "Then God [singular] said, 'Let Us [plural] make man in Our image...'" The Hebrew word translated as God here is *Elohim*, a plural noun. The Trinity or triunity of the Godhead (Father, Son, and Holy Spirit) is largely a New

Testament revelation, but it is first hinted at in the first chapter of the Bible.

Second we read, "'...and let them [plural] rule over the fish of the sea and over the birds of the sky and over the cattle and over all the earth, and over every creeping thing that creeps on the earth.'" It seems clear here that God's intent was that man be the crowning achievement of creation. There are two reasons why this is so:

1. Of all that God created, only man is in His image and likeness.
2. Man was to rule over all the earth.

Finally we read in verse 27, "And God created man in His own image, in the image of God He created him; male and female He created them." Verse 26 gives us God's intent. In verse 27 God performs His intent. In my mind, the "male and female" of this verse is linked to the plural "them" in the previous verse and applies to Adam and Eve. This gives "man" a generic meaning that includes both male and female, something that was commonly done until the last third of the twentieth century. ("Male and female" may have a broader meaning to include all of mankind, but that goes beyond the scope of our present discussion).

Genesis 1 gives us, in summary form, the story of creation. Chapter 2 fills in some of the details of the creation of Adam and Eve. For example, verse 7 tells us, "Then the Lord God formed man [Adam] of dust from the ground, and breathed into his nostrils the breath of life; and man became a living being." However, the creation of Eve was different:

So the Lord God caused a deep sleep to fall upon the man, and he slept; then He took one of his ribs, and closed up the flesh at that place. And the Lord God fashioned into a woman the rib which He had taken from the man, and brought her to the man. And the man said, "This is now bone of my bones, and flesh of my flesh; she shall be called Woman, because she was taken out of Man." (Genesis 2:21-23)

We will discuss the ramifications of this at a later time. For now, the objective is to show that Adam and Eve were created by God and that they (like the rest of God's creation) were created good and perfect and without fault or blemish of any kind, both physically and morally.

And God saw all that He had made, and behold, it was very good... (Genesis 1:31)

This is true because the essential goodness and perfection of God necessarily rules out His creation of anything which was not also good and perfect.

Another point crucial to our discussion is revealed in chapter 2:

8 And the Lord God planted a garden toward the east, in Eden...15 Then the Lord God took the man and put him into the garden of Eden to cultivate it and keep it. 16 And the Lord God commanded the man, saying, "From any tree of the garden you may eat freely; 17 but from the tree of the knowledge of good and evil you shall not eat, for in the day that you eat from it you shall surely die." (Genesis 2:8a, 15-17)

It is clear from the Bible (Genesis 2:17) that God created man with the power of choice and the mandate to choose.

Why is this clear? Because God gave man what can only be construed as a bona-fide choice whether or not to eat from the tree of the knowledge of good and evil.

Why is this important? Because given the moral capacity to choose, it is necessary that there be a point at which choice can be exercised—otherwise choice isn't really choice. Adam, by humbly submitting to God's prohibition at the tree, affirmed both his desire to please God (by not eating) and acknowledged that his very life depended on God (in the day that you eat from it you shall surely die). In this way Adam's love for God found tangible expression in the obedience of faith, and qualified him to be the recipient of the divine life as an agent of the divine will.

This subject often conjures up an image of the famous painting *Adam and Eve* by the German Renaissance artist Lucas Cranach. Here Eve is depicted as holding a piece of fruit (apparently an apple) and offering it to Adam. This may be where the idea of an apple being the so-called forbidden fruit came from. But that misses the point entirely. The significance is not in the fruit—apples, peaches, pears, or something else. The point is that God created man with the power of free choice. But choice without a place at which it can be exercised is no choice at all.

The important points coming out of this discussion are that:

- ➢ God created man.
- ➢ Man, as created, was perfect (good), both morally and in his physical being.
- ➢ God endowed man with the power of free choice and a mandate to choose.

The significance of these points will be seen as we proceed.

Your Adversary the Devil

3

Your Adversary, the Devil

I n chapter two the subject was creation: "In the beginning God created the heavens and the earth." It is important to understand that the beginning spoken of in Genesis 1 is the beginning of creation, not a beginning in itself. God had to exist before His creation, and the Bible is clear that the creation exists in the realm of time, which, in itself, exists in the realm of eternity—a period said to be without beginning or end; a period to which our concept of time would not apply.

It is not my purpose to attempt a study of eternity, other than to look briefly into what the Bible has to say about Satan in that dateless period before the creation.

There are two principal passages in the Bible that provide some background on Satan. These are Isaiah 14:12-20 and Ezekiel 28:11-19. Both of these writers were Old Testament prophets.

Who is Satan?

The Ezekiel 28 passage gives us the answer:

14 You were the anointed cherub who covers, and I placed you there. You were on the holy mountain of God; you walked in the midst of the stones of fire. 15 You were blameless in your ways from the day you were created, until

19

unrighteousness was found in you.

A cherub is an angel, one of at least two classes of angels listed in the Bible: cherubim and seraphim, although the indication is that there are more. Beyond being a cherub, he was *the anointed* cherub. Let's break this down: Grammatically, the word *the* is what is known as the definite article. The idea it conveys is, "the one and only." *Anointed* conveys the idea of coronation to high office. So Satan was not just *an* angel, he was *the* angel (with respect to his rank), and placed in that position by God.

Note also (verse 15), that Satan is a created being. Elsewhere in the Ezekiel passage the description given of him leaves no doubt that he was a magnificent character. Mind you, he was in no way equal to God, but he was blameless (perfect) in his ways—that is, until unrighteousness was found in him.

17 Your heart was lifted up because of your beauty; You corrupted your wisdom by reason of your splendor...

Proverbs 11:2 tells us, "When pride comes, then comes dishonor, But with the humble is wisdom." As can be seen here, the root of Satan's unrighteousness was pride. However, the specific sin coming out of that pride is more clearly outlined in Satan's five "I wills" that are documented in the Isaiah passage:

1. I will ascend to heaven.
2. I will raise my throne above the stars of God.
3. I will sit on the mount of assembly in the recesses of the north.
4. I will ascend above the heights of the clouds.
5. I will make myself like the Most High.

There is much that could be said about these five "I wills," but what it comes down to is an attack by Satan on the throne of God. This is briefly stated in the last "I will" (Isaiah 14:14): "...I will make myself like the Most High." Again looking at the grammar, the definite article tells us there can be one and *only* one Most High. But even if you remove the article, the word "Most"— meaning to the greatest or highest degree—tells us there can be only one. So the purpose of Satan to become like the Most High is nothing less than an attempt to dethrone Almighty God.

The Bible identifies angels as spirit beings, and the evidence is that Satan had a position that put him over a large number of other spirit beings (angels), many of whom fell with him in his rebellion against God. These, as differentiated from the holy angels, became the demons who function as Satan's underlings to this day.

What Happened?

It seems clear from the biblical record that Satan lost his exalted position in heaven. However, he was not cast down to the earth in the sense that his access to heaven is denied. The fall of Satan was a moral fall, not a fall that confined him to earth. Neither is there any biblical evidence for the idea that Satan or any of his underlings are now occupying hell. This is not to say that Satan will not be cast down to the earth or ultimately cast into the lake of fire, but to say that these things are reserved for a time yet future, as described in Revelation 12:7-9 and 20:10, respectively.

For the time being his position is in heaven; a position from which he has access both to God and to the earth. There is no evidence of any fellowship or agreement between God and Satan, but God, for His own sovereign purposes, permits this as well as Satan's activities (cf. Job 2:2, Revelation 12:10).

At this point, it is important to emphasize again that Satan is a created being—in no way equal to God. He is intelligent and, having had the opportunity to observe humans from creation until today, can predict with accuracy how humans will react in various situations. However, he does not possess all knowledge (omniscience) as God does. There is no evidence of an ongoing "battle of the ages" in which the outcome is unsure. Satan is ultimately under the authority of Jesus Christ and will be dealt with by Him at the proper time.

What are His Activities?

Satan's activities flow out of his purpose, which is mainly to raise his throne above the stars of God. To do this he must establish his authority and gain a kingdom for himself. This kingdom is spiritual in nature, he has been working to build it since the dawn of creation, and his work will continue until he is finally taken out of the way. The apostle Peter writes, "...Your adversary, the devil, prowls about like a roaring lion, seeking someone to devour" (1 Peter 5:8). He's intelligent and merciless and he wants your soul...and mine, and as many others as he can get in the time he has left.

To accomplish his purpose, he is not above using whatever means are at his disposal, including terror. From the Isaiah passage, speaking of Satan's judgment:

16 ...Is this the man [one] who made the earth tremble, who shook kingdoms, 17 who made the world like a wilderness and overthrew its cities, who did not allow his prisoners to go home?

However, his main tool appears to be deception. Jesus said of him, "...there is no truth in him. Whenever he speaks a lie, he speaks from his own nature; for he is a liar, and the father of lies" (John 8:44). Added to this, he is a master of craftiness, confusion, distortion, and subtlety. These are the devices he employs to deceive the unsuspecting into believing that what he is offering is good and desirable when, in reality, it is designed to make them his prisoners. This is an important point because even though Satan's end is in the lake of fire, he still gains a victory of sorts in that those whom he has deceived suffer the same fate as he. This, of course, is the ultimate deception.

Satan is God's enemy and mankind's enemy because his intent is to keep mankind from God. Thus he attempts to fulfill what is in reality a two-fold mission: to raise his throne above the stars of God and to thwart God's gracious plan for mankind. We'll talk more about this plan as we proceed.

Names of Satan

Isaiah 12:12 in the King James Version reads, "How art thou fallen from heaven, O Lucifer, son of the morning..." The meaning of *Lucifer* is son or star of the morning. I mention this here because Lucifer is a commonly known name for Satan. He is also known by a variety of other names in the Bible: Beelzebub, Belial, Devil, Dragon, the great red dragon, the evil one, and the serpent. Each of these names is indicative of some facet of his diabolical activity. It goes beyond the scope of our discussion to enter into a study of the meanings of these names, except to point out that when you see them in the Bible you'll know they refer to Satan.

The important points coming out of this discussion are:

➢ Satan is a fallen angel (a spirit being).
➢ Satan has underlings (demons) who assist him in his activities.
➢ Satan is the enemy of God.
➢ Satan is mankind's (your) enemy, desiring to keep you from God.
➢ Satan is smart and cruel and will do whatever is necessary to obtain his goals.
➢ Satan often uses deception and subtlety to achieve his ends.

What Happened?

4

What Happened?

When we left Adam and Eve in Genesis 2, they were newly-created persons in a newly-created world. Our detour in the last chapter was necessary to help us understand what takes place in Genesis 3.

The indication is that a certain amount of time elapsed between Genesis chapters 2 and 3. How much time is unknown, but it was apparently enough time for a relationship to develop between Adam and Eve, and enough time for Eve to have known about the prohibition God gave to Adam (before she was created) about eating from the tree. However, the evidence is clear that Eve had not yet borne children, nor was she pregnant.

Satan, in the guise of a serpent, approaches Eve with what seems an innocent question:

> Now the serpent was more crafty than any beast of the field which the Lord God had made. And he [the serpent] said to the woman, "Indeed, has God said, 'You shall not eat from any tree of the garden'?" (Genesis 3:1)

A number of questions could be raised at this point, not least of which is: Were animals able to speak in those days? The answer is unknown, except to say that the Bible does not record Eve registering surprise that a serpent spoke to her—which is not to say that she didn't. The Bible, while giving us the information we need, does not give the answer to every possible question. A better question might be, "Why approach Eve and not Adam?" This is something we'll discuss as we proceed. But here we see Satan drawing Eve in by misquoting God's command as if it were a prohibition against eating from *any* tree, as opposed to a single tree, the tree of the knowledge of good and evil.

The picture presented is one of Eve being alone, perhaps some distance away from her husband and possibly even near the tree in question. We see her response:

2 And the woman said to the serpent, "From the fruit of the trees of the garden we may eat; 3 but from the fruit of the tree which is in the middle of the garden, God has said, 'You shall not eat from it or touch it, lest you die.'"

Notice that Eve is inaccurate in her understanding of the prohibition. God had not commanded that the tree not be touched—though that wasn't necessarily a bad idea. One who would be saved from harm would do well to stay out of harm's way. She also softened the threat in God's warning from, "...in the day that you eat from it you shall surely die" to, "...lest you die." God's statement is one of cause and rapid effect: you eat from that tree, you die the same day. Eve's understanding removes the closeness of the effect from its cause. It also lessens its impact from being absolutely sure to, "for fear of" (which is the basic meaning of "lest").

I don't want to be too hard on Eve. The command was given to Adam before Eve was created, and there is no evidence to suggest that God gave it again directly to her. Of course, this does not excuse her. Clearly she knew of God's command. But she, not having heard it directly from God, was probably an easier target for Satan than Adam would have been. And make no mistake: Satan's real target was Adam.

There's a warning here for the unsuspecting: Satan often delivers temptations via unsuspected sources. A direct attack on Adam probably wouldn't have worked, but

What Happened?

Satan was able to get to him through someone he loved—his wife.

In verses 4 and 5 we find Satan flatly contradicting God, even to the point of more nearly using God's own words than Eve did:

> 4 And the serpent said to the woman, "You surely shall not die! 5 For God knows that in the day you eat from it your eyes will be opened, and you will be like God, knowing good and evil."

On the one hand, he calls God a liar. On the other, he misrepresents God's motives as being evil in seeking to withhold from her (them) something that would so obviously be beneficial. Your eyes will be opened and you'll realize that you are as God Himself—equal to God. You'll be kings and no longer subjects. You'll be self-sufficient and no longer dependent. Sound familiar? This is the mindset that caused Satan to fall.

Notice Eve's response:

> 6 When the woman saw that the tree was good for food, and that it was a delight to the eyes, and that the tree was desirable to make one wise, she took from its fruit and ate; and she gave also to her husband with her, and he ate.

She *saw*. She should have turned her eyes away, but by looking with pleasure on the forbidden fruit she fell into temptation. Much that causes us to sin comes in by the eyes.

She *took*. Satan did not pluck it off the tree and put it in her hand. She took it of her own volition. Satan can tempt, but he cannot force.

She *ate*. Maybe she didn't intend to eat when she first looked, but sin is always a slippery slope—before you know it you're past the point of no return. The wisest thing is to be alert and not get involved in the first place.

She *gave also to her husband with her*. The way the text reads, it is probable that Adam was not with her when she first encountered the serpent, but came into the situation

29

later, perhaps as she was eating. Perhaps she handed him the same piece of fruit she had tasted. Maybe she even told him how good it was. The text doesn't say. However, one thing was sure: she had not dropped over dead.

He ate. Overcome, perhaps, by his love for Eve he accepted the fruit from her hand and ate. Eve was deceived by the serpent (1 Timothy 2:14), but Adam could make no such claim. He did not have a corrupt nature to betray him, or a bad upbringing, or live in less-than-desirable circumstances. He acted in deliberate disobedience to God and fell into sin. And died. And Eve fell. And died.

Oh, they didn't drop over dead. That's part of the satanic genius behind this: they didn't die physically, they died spiritually. Adam lived to be 930-years-old, but every day from that day until the day he physically died he lived as a dead man.

This is what Satan was after. The command not to eat had been given by God to Adam. Adam was the responsible party in this. Woman was made by God for man, "...a helper suitable for him" (Genesis 2:20). God gave headship to the man by order of creation, as the apostle Paul argues in 1 Corinthians 11:3-12. When God cursed the ground because of Adam (Genesis 3:17), He did it, "Because you have *listened to the voice of your wife*, and have eaten from the tree about which I commanded you, saying, 'You shall not eat from it;'..." (emphasis added).

This is not to denigrate women, but simply to state the facts as they are recorded in Scripture. Headship is more a responsibility than an opportunity to exert power. As far as the marriage relationship is concerned, men would do well to remember that woman was not taken from man's foot— to be trodden down by him. Nor was she taken from his head—to dominate him. She was taken from his side—to be an equal. She was taken from under his arm—to be protected. She was taken from near his heart—to be loved.

Adam and Eve had to decide whether God or Satan was lying. They decided God was. They found out He wasn't.

I take away from this another warning: The most convincing lies are lies that contain a measure of truth. It is clear, though not stated up front, that the death about which God was speaking is spiritual death. The death about which Satan was speaking was physical death. Adam and Eve did not drop over from eating the fruit, but they died just the same. Satan is the master deceiver. You trifle with him at your own peril.

All death is separation. Physical death is separation from the physical world. Spiritual death is separation from God.

And Man Became a Living Soul

5

And Man Became a Living Soul

Most people, including some theologians, regard man as consisting of two parts: a body and a soul. The body is the material part of man (consisting of visible matter); the soul is the non-material part—the unseen part of man that survives the death of the body. The Bible recognizes this as well. For example, Jesus said, "And do not fear those who kill the body, but are unable to kill the soul; but rather fear Him who is able to destroy both soul and body in hell" (Matthew 10:28).

There is much that could be said on this topic, but it would quickly go beyond the scope of our discussion. For now I'm suggesting that this is a shorthand way to speak of man as having both material and non-material existence. I say this because the Bible elsewhere explicitly depicts man as consisting of three parts. The apostle Paul, writing under the inspiration of the Holy Spirit, says this in 1 Thessalonians 5:23 (emphasis added):

Now may the God of peace Himself sanctify you entirely; and may your *spirit and soul and body* be preserved complete, without blame at the coming of our Lord Jesus Christ.

Recall that God made man in His image. Since God is a Trinity (Father, Son, and Holy Spirit), it follows that man would also be triune in nature (spirit, soul, and body).

The body is the part we're most familiar with—seeing as we all have one. It is our interface with the physical world; the means by which we gather information, communicate, and give expression to our souls. The Bible describes it as our house, our earthly tent or tabernacle: "For we know that if the earthly tent which is our house is torn down, we have a building from God, a house not made with hands, eternal in the heavens" (2 Corinthians 5:1). If we look closely at this verse we get the idea. The word "our" in the phrase "our house" pictures a place where someone lives. That someone is *our* non-material self. The word "tent" conveys the idea of a temporary dwelling, meaning that our non-material self is not always going to live there.

The word "soul," as it is used in the creation account, is a very interesting word. In Genesis 1:30, speaking of the animal kingdom, we read: "...to every beast of the earth and to every bird of the sky and to every thing that moves on the earth which has life [literally, in which is a living soul], I have given every green plant for food..." In Genesis 2:7, speaking of man, we read: "Then the Lord God formed man of dust from the ground, and breathed into his nostrils the breath of life; and man became a living being [literally, a living soul]." In both cases the Bible uses the same Hebrew word, *nephesh,* for soul. Does this mean that man is an animal? From a physiological standpoint, yes. That he is much more than an animal will, I trust, become apparent.

In the classic definition, the soul is also a tri-unity consisting of mind, will, and emotion; although some see it as the mind encompassing will and emotion. In either case it is important to point out that the word "mind" is not referring to the brain (a physical entity). Sir John Eccles, winner of the Nobel Prize for his work on brain research, described the brain as, "A machine that a ghost can operate." The ghost, to use Eccles' terminology, is the soul.

Ideas are not physical in nature. Good and evil, while they may give rise to physical acts, begin as thoughts.

Ethics and morals are things which everyone understands to some degree, but they have no physical substance. You cannot weigh truth, justice, or mercy; or describe the color or texture of love. Nevertheless, we admit to knowledge of all of these. Clearly, then, there is a link whereby the "ghost" is able to trigger neural activity in the brain, thus triggering physical activity in the man. Exactly how this link works is understood by God alone.

The soul is identified as the seat of behavior. And neither man nor animal needs any particular relationship with God simply to behave. Your dog understands love (in a doggie kind of way); and you can't top a dog when it comes to loyalty. And certainly dogs are more ethical than some people. So what is it that makes man more than just an animal?

God gave man the human spirit—something He did not give to any other created life. It is this spirit which differentiates man from animal.

The seat of the human spirit is the soul. The Bible makes the connection of soul and spirit and the distinction between them clear in Hebrews 4:12 (emphasis added):

For the word of God is living and active and sharper than any two-edged sword, and piercing as far as the division of *soul and spirit*, of both joints and marrow, and able to judge the thoughts and intentions of the heart.

So while the soul and spirit are in their essences distinct, together they form the non-material part of man, the part that gives life to your body, the part that makes you, you—the you that will survive endlessly after physical death.

The unique thing about the spirit of man is that it is the intended residence of the Spirit of God (the Holy Spirit). God inhabiting man. Certainly this was true of Adam in his innocence. Proverbs 20:27 tells us, "The spirit of man is the lamp of the Lord..." One way to picture this is as the spirit of man having in it a light bulb burning brightly, for: "...God is light, and in Him there is no darkness at all" (1

John 1:5). When Adam ate the fruit, God left him and turned off the light on His way out.

Man—created to be inhabited by God—now without God, died (spiritually) and was plunged into darkness.

Through One Man Sin Entered the World

6

Through One Man Sin Entered the World

All death is separation. When your soul/spirit separates from your body you are physically dead. When God separated Himself from Adam, Adam—though remaining physically alive and retaining his mind, will, and emotion—was spiritually dead.

Man, created to be inhabited by God, was reduced to the status of clever animal. But, as bad as that is, it gets worse. As a clever animal, man might have been as harmless as a pet rabbit—except for another principle which was at work. It is stated briefly by Jesus in John 8:34, "...everyone who commits sin is the slave of sin." Paul expands on this in Romans 6:16:

> Do you not know that when you present yourselves to someone as slaves for obedience, you are slaves of the one whom you obey, either of sin resulting in death, or of obedience resulting in righteousness?

John Bunyan, in his 1682 allegory *The Holy War,* pictured the soul of man as a town, which he called Mansoul. It is an interesting and apt figure of speech for our discussion.

Man, as created, had no "government" as such. Under the gracious influence of the Holy Spirit, Adam, by obedience, did those things which were good and pleasing in God's sight—until, by the exercise of his free choice, he ate the forbidden fruit and God left him.

Man's relationship with God, as we discussed in chapter two, had been one of dependence. The act of disobedience was an act of independence according to Satan's word, "...you will be like God..." Man, now empty of the one true God, became his own god, and Mansoul got its first king: Self.

This principle of self-rule is what the Bible calls the flesh. This is not to be confused with the body, except that it is indicative of a mindset intent on fulfilling bodily desires contrary to God's revealed will and often at the expense of others. It is the Me, Myself, and I mindset that makes me number one in my own eyes and in my attitudes toward others. It is the desire to be famous, to be well-known. It's the mindset that makes me sure that I'm better than most others or even some others; the mindset that allows me to hurt others either physically or emotionally, etc. Some translations call it the "sinful mind" or "sinful nature." It is also known as "sin" (the motivating principle) as opposed to "sins" (the acts), the "natural man," the "old man," "self" or "old self," and perhaps by other names as well. The problem is that Self is under the influence of Satan because, "...when you present yourselves to someone as slaves for obedience, you are slaves of the one whom you obey..." So Self has been a corrupt enterprise since the day he took over. Adam's son Cain killed his own brother Abel, and things have been going down hill ever since.

"Adam's son? Wait a minute. Are you saying that this spiritual death business is passed on from generation to generation?"

Yes. The Bible makes that very clear. Paul again, from Romans 5:12:

Therefore, just as through one man [Adam] sin entered into the world, and death through sin, and so death spread to all men...

The curious may wish to know how this takes place. However, the Bible, while stating the fact of the matter, does not present the mechanism by which it occurs. Men have sought to figure this out for a long time and have advanced various theories, often complex and sometimes bizarre, to define what theologians call Inherited Sin. But if you ask the wrong question you can't help but arrive at an erroneous conclusion. Perhaps rather than asking what occurs, a better question might be what doesn't occur?

Inherited sin is really a misnomer. We'll discuss sin more as we proceed, but for now, in order to grasp this we need to ask what sin is. In the basic sense, sin is any want or lack of conformity to God's righteousness; this is minimally expressed in the Bible in the Moral Law—the Ten Commandments. Therefore sin, being lack of conformity, is not a thing in itself that can be passed genetically from generation to generation like red hair or blue eyes (which occasionally skip generations).

What is "passed" is spiritual death; and even that is a misnomer because one cannot pass what one does not possess—spiritual life, the life of God. So every person born after Adam's fall (which is every person ever born) has been born spiritually dead, ruled by Self, and under the influence of Satan.

In this condition the only option left, apart from getting God back inside the person, is sin. The reason why this is so is perhaps best illustrated by an incident that occurred when Jesus walked on the earth: One day a young man ran up to Jesus and asked him, "Good Teacher, what shall I do to inherit eternal life?" (Mark 10:17). You would think that Jesus would have given him some deep, philosophical answer; but instead He replied, "Why do you call Me good? No one is good except God alone" (verse 18).

This is a wonderful passage that, among other things, juxtaposes the divinity and humanity of Christ, but the point the Lord was making to this fellow is that man does not possess a goodness of his own. The only *real* goodness that a person can possess is goodness derived from God, who alone is good. But man is empty of God and therefore empty of the only possible goodness he can possess. All that's left to him is sin:

43

...There is none righteous, not even one; there is none who understands, there is none who seeks for God; all have turned aside, together they have become useless; there is none who does good, there is not even one. (Romans 3:10-12)

Obviously, as human beings, we have a sense of good and bad, right and wrong, and certainly much good is done in this world. But the goodness possessed by the natural man is always relative to his fellow human beings; and while it might provide beneficial outcomes for mankind, it does not measure up to the standard of God's righteousness. Therefore even our "good" deeds, when seen from this perspective, are sin; for "...whatever is not from faith is sin." (Romans 14:23b).

So sin is not inherited in any organic sense. It is the result of the condition man finds himself in as a consequence of the fall.

The Right of Conquest

Recall from Genesis 1:26 that God gave man rule over all the earth (which, by the way, included the serpent). Satan, in securing Adam's obedience, legitimately gained that rule from man and installed himself as earth's ruler. This is what is known as Right of Conquest. It is an ancient principle, even observed in international law, although it has fallen out of favor somewhat since the end of World War II. The basic idea is that "to the victor belong the spoils"—the victor, in this case, being Satan and the spoils being rule of the earth, which, by Right of Creation, still belongs to God.

The Bible, while it doesn't spell this out specifically, acknowledges it in the titles that it gives to Satan: god of this world, ruler of this world, prince of this world, etc.

This is actually double-trouble for man because not only is he now without God, but he has moved from the paradise of the Garden of Eden into a world that is hostile to him.

This also gives Satan a real foothold in his bid to keep man from God because now, at least to a certain extent, he controls the environment in which man lives.

Satan's assault on man is primarily through temptation, and temptations fall into three basic categories: the lust of the flesh, the lust of the eyes, and the pride of life (1 John 2:15-17). This was how he deceived Eve: She saw that the tree was "good for food" (lust of the flesh), and that it was "a delight to the eyes" (lust of the eyes), and that the tree was "desirable to make one wise" (the pride of life).

At the dawn of creation, Satan had not yet gained a kingdom of influencers because Adam and Eve were the only two people on the earth. Therefore, he was forced to use a direct, frontal assault in his successful bid to influence our first parents. Over the course of time, however, his kingdom of influencers has grown ponderously large and he is no longer obliged to operate in a direct way.[1]

These days it seems like his main weapon of influence is entertainment. This would include entertainment in all of its current forms: movies, television, radio, various web sites, books, types of music, etc. I hasten to point out that this is not intended to be a flat condemnation of these media—obviously they can be put to good as well as evil uses, and often are. But it is to say that, in general, entertainment appears to be his current weapon of choice; the medium through which he promotes profligate lifestyles and ways of thinking as the normal way of life.

While much of what is presented in these media is in opposition to God's revealed will, it is presented in such a way as to make it appealing, fun, glamorous, and to be emulated, when in reality it is a veiled enticement to sin. Godliness or godly ways of thinking, if portrayed at all, are defined by these influencers. And those portrayed as "the godly" are usually portrayed as out-of-touch, irrelevant, ridiculous, insincere, lacking in credibility, or even criminal. Generally though, if you hear the name of God or Jesus uttered at all it is in the form of invective.

The influence this exerts is huge—particularly on the immature and less astute. By presenting evil as good and good as evil (cf. Isaiah 5:20), Satan is able to build his kingdom by subtly persuading people to act in opposition to God's will (sin) and to avoid at all costs the embarrassment of any association with God. It is a masterstroke of satanic genius whereby he appears to be offering people complete freedom when in reality what he is offering them is bondage to sin—a bondage from which they will ultimately perish.

Make no mistake: the Bible identifies a subset of mankind as "...those who are perishing" (2 Corinthians 4:3). Just what percentage this subset includes is not stated, but the indication is that the number is large—so large that it would be grammatically more correct to say that the subset consists of those who are *not* perishing:

> Enter by the narrow gate; for the gate is wide, and the way is broad that leads to destruction, and many are those who enter by it. For the gate is small, and the way is narrow that leads to life, and few are those who find it. (Matthew 7:13-14)

You could argue that most people don't know this, and certainly that would include those that produce entertainment. Nevertheless, it is fair to say as a general rule that much of what passes for entertainment nowadays is produced by those who are perishing for those who are perishing to keep those who are perishing in Satan's kingdom.

None of this happened overnight, but slowly over the course of time—little by little until what is accepted without question or complaint as entertainment in these media today, would be considered shocking and outrageous if it suddenly appeared in the media of 50 years ago.

Why is this so? The answer, in a word, is *corruption,* and the principle is found in Romans 6:19: "...you presented your members as slaves to impurity and to lawlessness, resulting in further lawlessness..." Law, in this context, is broadly indicative of the entire revealed will of God. The idea being conveyed is that impurity and lawlessness introduce corruption into the soul. Corruption hardens the heart and leads to more of the same, which corrupts the soul even more. And the cycle continues. It's a matter of influence. The more you are influenced by those more corrupt than yourself, the more corrupt you yourself become.

Because of this, things that would have been almost universally condemned as grievous sins in that day pass unchallenged as entertainment today. And our hearts get harder and harder. And Satan knows that the harder your heart gets the more difficult it is for you to hear the voice of God. And therein lies man's problem and Satan's potential victory.

Understanding the default

The meaning of the word "default" has changed somewhat over the course of time. While it still retains its original meaning as a failure to do something, in the computer age it has come to mean what you get if you *don't* do something. My word processor has the default font Times New Roman. If I open the program and start typing, I don't have to do anything special to get Times New Roman because it's the default. If I don't like the outcome provided by the default, I'm free to change it to something I do like, for example Courier or Palatino.

The same is true in the spiritual realm, and the reason this is important is because spiritual death affects succeeding generations. You "inherited" it from your parents, who "inherited" it from their parents, and on up the line until it eventually gets back to Adam. Your particular Mansoul or Womansoul came with its own king already installed. That king is Self, and Self is that sin principle that is resident in every person. By default, every child born physically alive since Adam has been born spiritually dead (empty of God).

Worse, because Self is motivated by Satan, sin (the principle) is the instigator of sins (the acts) in every person. We were all born to it and it affects everyone, "for all have sinned and fall short of the glory of God" (Romans 3:23).

At least 20 different words are translated as *sin* in the Bible, so arriving at a simple definition is difficult. Lawlessness, as stated above, is a good definition as long as it is seen in its broadest sense as a departure from any of God's standards. However, the most common definition of sin in the New Testament is "missing the mark." That's the meaning of "sinned" in the Romans 3:23 reference above. The picture is of an arrow falling short of its target. However, it is not just passively missing the right mark. It is actively hitting the wrong mark—every shot arrow hits something. Neither is it missing the bullseye by mistake, with the idea that if I keep trying I'll eventually hit it.

The two words "fall short" are a single word in the original Greek; a present tense verb which, in Greek grammar, denotes continuous action. So the concept here is continually falling short; that is, try as you might, you can *never* hit the target—nobody can, "for *all* have sinned..." Of course, this assumes that you're even aiming at the glory of God. I fear most people are not. But even if you are, this negates the idea that a person can find favor with God if his or her good deeds somehow outweigh the bad. Jesus said, "...you are to be perfect, as your heavenly Father is perfect" (Matthew 5:48).

The standard is perfection. However, you, along with everyone else, are born spiritually dead (empty of God) and ruled by Self, that sin principle (motivated by Satan) which inspires your lawless acts and missing the mark (sins).

Sin is a horrendous thing in the sight of holy God. The Old Testament prophet Habakkuk perhaps said it best: "Thine eyes are too pure to approve evil, And Thou canst not look on wickedness with favor..." (Habakkuk 1:13).

In the Old Testament God, speaking through the prophet Ezekiel, said: "Behold, all souls are Mine; the soul of the father as well as the soul of the son is Mine. The soul who sins will die" (Ezekiel 18:4). In the New Testament, God said through the apostle Paul, "...the wages of sin is death..." (Romans 6:23).

The death about which God is speaking is not physical death, which is common to all people. It is what the Bible refers to as the Second Death in Revelation 20:11-15:

11 And I saw a great white throne and Him who sat upon it, from whose presence earth and heaven fled away, and no place was found for them. 12 And I saw the dead, the great and the small, standing before the throne, and books were opened; and another book was opened, which is the book of life; and the dead were judged from the things which were written in the books, according to their deeds. 13 And the sea gave up the dead which were in it, and death and Hades gave up the dead which were in them; and they were judged, every one of them according to their deeds. 14 And death and Hades were thrown into the lake of fire. This is the second death, the lake of fire. 15 And if anyone's name was not found written in the book of life, he was thrown into the lake of fire.

The lake of fire (verse 14) is the second death about which God is speaking. It is the place that is popularly called hell. According to Revelation 20:10, those who go there "...will be tormented day and night forever and ever."

This is the default—what you get if you don't do something.

---

1. Influence is the capacity to mold or sway belief or opinion. Influencers, for the purpose of this discussion, are people who do Satan's bidding. To a certain degree, this includes everyone. Because we are all born spiritually dead, we are all under the influence of Satan; not necessarily in a personal way, but under the influence of a world-system motivated and dominated by satanic ideals. "...the whole world lies in the power of the evil one [Satan]" (1 John 5:19).

Some people are in his kingdom, but only because they were born into it. Others are deeply in his kingdom by their own choices (robbers, murderers, drug dealers, pornographers, etc.). Most fall somewhere in between. This represents the norm in the fallen world. Consequently, people typically do not recognize that they are in Satan's kingdom, that they are being influenced, or that they are, in turn, influencing others. Even those who seek to influence others typically do not recognize this. Nor do any of us realize the far-reaching effects of our influence: who we influence, who that person influences, who the third person influences, and on down the line. This is one reason why God has reserved judgment until the end of time (Revelation 20:11-15). It's pretty scary to think that you can be held at least partially responsible for what someone does perhaps decades after you die.

Religion, by itself, cannot deliver you from Satan's kingdom. Ancient Israel was a particularly religious society and of all the people perhaps the most religious was a group known as the Pharisees. It was to them that Jesus said, "You are of your father the devil, and you want to do the desires of your father..." (John 8:44). Only Jesus can deliver you from Satan's kingdom, and only by your choice.

Sin and the Law

7

Sin and the Law

To gain a better understanding of sin it is important to look at the Law of God. This law is embodied in what is commonly known as the Ten Commandments or Decalogue. They appear in Exodus 20:3-17:

1. You shall have no other gods before Me.
2. You shall not make for yourself an idol, or any likeness of what is in heaven above or on the earth beneath or in the water under the earth. You shall not worship them or serve them; for I, the Lord your God, am a jealous God, visiting the iniquity of the fathers on the children, on the third and the fourth generations of those who hate Me, but showing lovingkindness to thousands, to those who love Me and keep My commandments.
3. You shall not take the name of the Lord your God in vain, for the Lord will not leave him unpunished who takes His name in vain.
4. Remember the sabbath day, to keep it holy. Six days you shall labor and do all your work, but the seventh day is a sabbath of the Lord your God; in it you shall not do any work, you or your son or your daughter, your male or your female servant or your cattle or your sojourner who stays with you. For in six days the Lord made the heavens and the earth,

the sea and all that is in them, and rested on the seventh day; therefore the Lord blessed the sabbath day and made it holy.

5. Honor your father and your mother, that your days may be prolonged in the land which the Lord your God gives you.
6. You shall not murder.
7. You shall not commit adultery.
8. You shall not steal.
9. You shall not bear false witness against your neighbor.
10. You shall not covet your neighbor's house; you shall not covet your neighbor's wife or his male servant or his female servant or his ox or his donkey or anything that belongs to your neighbor.

Those familiar with the Bible may recognize these commandments as being the legal code given by God, through Moses, to the nation of Israel. But, of course, they existed in the mind of the immutable God from before the foundation of the world. Therefore, the moral principles that the Law embodies are eternal. There never was a time nor will be a time when they do not represent the will of God for mankind.

Whole books have been written on the meaning and application of the Commandments, so there is much that could be said about them. However, my purpose is not to enter into a study of the Law, but to make a few observations and to point out the purpose for which it was given.

The purpose of any law, generally speaking, is to restrain behavior by codifying those behaviors which are considered unacceptable and prescribing the penalty to be incurred should one engage in any of those behaviors. The Law of God does this and violation of this law is, by definition, sin.

In chapter one, we spoke of the so-called natural law as being "how we innately know when what we or others are doing is wrong." The Commandments put names on those acts (sins): stealing, lying, murder, etc; and the penalty prescribed for sin is death: "The soul who sins will die."

As you begin to understand the Commandments it becomes clear that you cannot break just one of them. The first commandment, "You shall have no other gods before Me," portrays God as the absolute Sovereign, prohibits the worship of many gods (polytheism) or any other single (supposed) god. But its meaning goes deeper to include anything or anyone we would put in the place of God. Most often that is Self. So if I break the eighth commandment by stealing, I'm also breaking the first commandment by putting myself before God, who told me not to steal. The same is true for all the commandments as well as for things not specifically written in the Law: spouse, children, money, job, sex, politics, environment, etc. All of these things are in and of themselves good, but if they're more important to me than God they're sin.

I may offend or otherwise hurt my neighbor, and that may constitute sin. However, if I do sin it is always and only against God. This is true because God, as man's creator, is the only One vested with the right to lay down the rules for man's behavior; and the only One able to enforce the penalty of the second death (cf. Psalm 51:4).

There is also a spiritual dimension to the Law. For example, Jesus said: "You have heard that it was said, 'You shall not commit adultery'; but I say to you, that everyone who looks on a woman to lust for her has committed adultery with her already in his heart" (Matthew 5:27-28). In the same context He equated hatred with murder. Every act begins in the mind and Jesus made it clear that unrighteous thoughts are sins (cf. Isaiah 55:7).

If you look carefully at the Commandments and are honest with yourself, you'll have to admit that you've broken most of them repeatedly since your youth. You cannot keep the Law—nobody can.

The purpose of the Law

In 2 Corinthians 3, Paul refers to the Law as "...the ministry of death, in letters engraved on stones..." (verse

7), and "...the ministry of condemnation..." (verse 9). The Law condemns its offenders to death; and this includes everyone because no one is able to keep the Law.

So why even make a law if all it can do is condemn? Because the Law, on the one hand, gives us a picture of the righteousness of God; so when Jesus says, "you are to be perfect, as your heavenly Father is perfect," it helps us see how far short we fall of that standard. On the other hand, it gives to sin the character of transgression (violation of known ordinances), as we discussed above, by putting names on sins. Sin was in the world before the Law came in, but sin was not credited to people as transgression when there was no law. Nevertheless, death reigned from Adam to Moses (to whom God gave the Law) because man is spiritually dead (empty of God), as Paul explains in Romans 5:13-14.

You wouldn't think so, but this is a great blessing to man because characterizing sin as transgression gives man the awareness that he has transgressed, and therein lies the objective of the Law. The awareness of our transgressions coupled with the awareness of our inability to keep the Law is designed to demonstrate to us the absolute futility of attempting to gain acceptance with God based on keeping the Law or on any kind of good works we might do—even religious good works. "...whatever the Law says, it speaks to those within the Law, so that every mouth may be stopped, and all the world be under judgment to God. Because by the works of the Law no flesh will be justified before Him—for through the Law is the full knowledge of sin" (Romans 3:19-20, literal).

So what's the point in having the whole world guilty before God? "...the Scripture has shut up all men under sin, that the promise by faith in Jesus Christ might be given to those who believe" (Galatians 3:22). Acceptance with God is not on the basis of keeping the Law or of good works of any kind, but on the basis of faith—of believing in Jesus Christ. The Law, then, "...has become our tutor to lead us to Christ, that we may be justified by faith" (Galatians 3:24).

The Law and Judgment

At some point every person will face God's judgment. How you come out of that judgment is, in some respects, a function of when you face it. In the end, it comes down to Christ or the Law. If you realize that your sins have condemned you to death and that there is nothing you can do on your own to change that, you may voluntarily enter into judgment with God and be acquitted by believing in Jesus Christ: "For Christ is the end [fulfillment] of the law for righteousness to everyone who believes" (Romans 10:4). The effect of this is that your name will be permanently entered into the book of life.

On the other hand, you can refuse to believe that you are a sinner and that your sins have condemned you to death. If that is the case, you will face God's judgment at the end of time, be judged out of the Law, and consigned to the lake of fire: "And I saw the dead, the great and the small, standing before the throne, and books were opened; and another book was opened, which is the book of life; and the dead were judged from the things which were written in the books, according to their deeds... and if anyone's name was not found written in the book of life, he was thrown into the lake of fire" (Revelation 20:12, 15).

What in the World is God Up To?

8

What in the World is God Up To?

The preceding few chapters have painted what can only be called a sad picture. So is God, after creating a perfect universe, up in heaven hitting His hand against His forehead and saying, "What was I thinking?"

No. God is omniscient. This means that God possesses perfect knowledge. He does not need to learn anything. He has never learned anything and, indeed, cannot learn because He already knows. In the Old Testament, the prophet Isaiah poses a rhetorical question (a question not expecting an answer because the answer is universally known):

Who has directed the Spirit of the Lord, or as His counselor has informed Him? With whom did He consult and who gave Him understanding? And who taught Him in the path of justice and taught Him knowledge, and informed Him of the way of understanding? (Isaiah 40:13-14)

In the New Testament, Paul poses a similar question in Romans 11:34 and the understood answer in both cases is *nobody*. To suppose otherwise would be to suppose God as being less than Himself: the Almighty, the Most High God, maker of heaven and earth and all that is.

We also know that God's omniscience is tied to His immutability (His unchangeableness). God says of Himself in Malachi 3:6: "For I, the Lord, do not change..." For God to learn anything would be for Him to change in some way, which is impossible.

God knows all things perfectly. He never discovers anything. He never wonders about anything. He is never surprised or amazed. So we can say with complete confidence that God knew all about Satan's rebellion and fall before He ever created him. We can also say that God knew all about Adam's fall and the effect it would have on the world and mankind down through the ages before He ever created the earth and man. And He knew what He would do about it; for He knows the end from the beginning—nothing that has happened or ever will happen escapes His perfect knowledge.

So, what in the world is God up to?

Nowadays it is common for organizations to have a purpose statement—an explicit statement making clear the objective they're aiming at. The Bible does not give us a direct answer as to God's purpose in creation. However, it does tell us about the God who created and from that we can figure out His purpose.

Why would we want to understand God's purpose in creation? Because God did not create man just to ultimately consign him to the lake of fire. Remember that man is the crowning achievement of creation, made in God's own image and likeness. God *knew* that Adam would sin and through that sin he and mankind would fall. And because God knew it would happen, He *expected* it to happen. And because He knew and expected it *before* He created man, it is fair to say that He *wanted* it to happen.[1]

That's right, He wanted it to happen.

The question is, why? And failure to ask this question has led men, in some cases, to propound doctrines that misrepresent and actually malign God's integrity and character. So asking the question and getting the right answer is critical to seeing God as He really is and understanding what He is doing.

We understand God (to the extent that we can) by those things which He has revealed as being true about Himself. We call these things the attributes of God, and we've already touched on a couple of them: omniscience and immutability. Among His many other attributes are grace, justice, love, and mercy. It would be incorrect to think of these as things or as qualities possessed by God. They are God's nature, how He is in His essence: God shows mercy because He is merciful, justice because He is just, love because He is love. God cannot be unmerciful, unjust, or unloving, etc. because to do so would make Him less than Himself, and that is not possible because God is immutable. Therefore, God does not suspend one attribute to exercise another, i.e., love does not override justice. If it did, God would be less than Himself and neither loving nor just. God is perfect in love and perfect in justice as He is in all of His attributes.

We say that "...God is love" (1 John 4:8). But for love to be something more than merely theoretical or potential, it requires an object—something or someone to love. This "someone," I believe, was God's motivation in the creation of man. This does not indicate a need on God's part, because there is perfect love among the Trinity. However, it does indicate God's desire to extend that love outside of Himself. And that is a key point: this whole thing is about love.

Understand that God could have made man without giving him the power of free choice. However, to do so would be to create an automaton—a robot. And a robot could not truly accept love or truly return it. Any love offered to such a creature would be unanswered and love would remain in the realm of the theoretical. So we see the necessity for love to have a relational component if it is to be valid. A man might love a woman, but if the woman is incapable of loving the man in return the man's love is of no value to her. Neither is it of any value to the man, being unrequited. He might as well love a fence post. So love, in order to be valid in any real sense, requires the power of free choice in both parties.

63

Apart from the fall of man, most of the attributes of God would never be understood. Grace, justice, love, and mercy (among God's other attributes) would have no need of expression in an unfallen world. The result would be that we could never really know God.

It was never God's plan to have ongoing fellowship with Adam and Eve in the Garden of Eden. So the fall of man did not foil God's plan. Instead, it put God's plan of redeeming love into operation. And this is the key to God's purpose in creating man.

Whole theologies have been built on the idea that, before the foundation of the world, God chose (for no apparent reason) who will go to heaven and who will not. But in a world where choice is possible, this would be both unloving and unjust—making God less than Himself. Sending everyone to hell because of sin would be just, but it would be unloving—making God less than Himself. Sending everyone to heaven would be loving, but it would be unjust—again, making God less than Himself. It doesn't matter who you are, you can go to heaven—if you want to.

God's purpose in creating man is to call out a people for His own possession. As Moses said to Israel in Deuteronomy 4:20:

But the Lord has taken you and brought you out of the iron furnace, from Egypt, to be a people for His own possession...

So the apostle Paul said to Christians in Titus 2:14:

[Christ Jesus] who gave Himself for us, that He might redeem us from every lawless deed and purify for Himself a people for His own possession, zealous for good deeds.

And God is very much pro-choice in this matter. He is calling out people from this domain of darkness to be people for His own possession. But He only wants people to be His who want to be His. Therefore, He allows people to choose Him. By so doing He remains both loving and just and maintains integrity in His other attributes as well. In other words, God remains Himself.

Understand that this is about love; God is not calling out populations, He is calling out people—individuals to be the recipients of His love, who want that love and will love Him in return.

But there's a problem and the problem has never been about love; it has been about justice. On the one hand man is spiritually dead (empty of God), on the other he has sinned. And it might be better to say that he has amassed sins for he continually misses the mark. This has set the default end for every person to hell—the lake of fire. So the problem is: how can God let guilty sinners into heaven and at the same time remain just? Justice demands a penalty. The penalty is the second death—eternal separation from God—tormented day and night, forever and ever in the lake of fire. Unless the penalty is paid, God's justice cannot be satisfied. If God's justice is not satisfied, nobody gets into heaven because God cannot be less than Himself.

In order for God to recognize man as fit to be in His presence, He must "see" the Holy Spirit in the man. However, the Holy Spirit will not enter man because of sin—He will not live in a house that is unclean.

Therein lies the dilemma: God's justice is demanding a penalty be paid for sin, but the only way man can pay the penalty is to spend eternity in the lake of fire.

---

1. God's statement to Adam in Genesis 2:17, "'...but from the tree of the knowledge of good and evil you shall not eat, for in the day that you eat from it you shall surely die'" is often viewed as an if-then conditional statement: *if* you do that, *then* this will happen. However, if you carefully examine what God is saying: "...in the day that you eat from it..." you will see the statement anticipates the act.

It's fair to say that Adam did not, at that moment, intend to eat from the tree, and probably did not intend to do it right up until the time he did it. But God already knew it would happen, when it would happen, how it would happen, and everything about it.

Love Found a Way

9

Love Found a Way

Most people have at least heard about the virgin birth of Christ, which was, of course, a miraculous birth. The importance of this birth is that it bypasses the sin problem. The virgin birth of Christ puts on earth a man who, apart from His Godhood, was man as God intended man to be—a man like Adam before the fall. This is why Christ is referred to as the last Adam: "So also it is written, 'The first man, Adam, became a living soul.' The last Adam [Christ] became a life-giving spirit" (1 Corinthians 15:45). The virgin birth also assumes the corruption of man and his inability to deliver himself from that corruption: "For as in [the first] Adam all die, so also in Christ all shall be made alive" (1 Corinthians 15:22).

The significance of this lies in who Christ is and why He came to earth. Remember, God's justice demands a penalty be paid for sin—an eternal penalty, a penalty we could not pay. But God's love found a way to pay it. The apostle John gives us a glimpse into this love in 1 John 4:10:

In this is love, not that we loved God, but that He loved us and sent His Son to be the propitiation for our sins.

A propitiation (pro-pish-e-a-shen) is an atoning sacrifice. To atone is to satisfy God's justice, i.e., to pay the penalty. So here's what this verse is saying: We didn't love God, but

God loved (loves) us. We owed a penalty to God because of sin. However, it was a penalty we could not pay apart from being tormented day and night forever and ever in the lake of fire. God, in love, determined that He Himself would pay the penalty for us. Jesus Christ, God the Son, sacrificed Himself for us—actually dying for us on a Roman cross—going into the place of death on our behalf. That sacrificial act of Christ on our behalf satisfied God's justice, making it possible for God to forgive our sins and at the same time remain just.

It may seem extreme to you that God had to become a man to pay the penalty for our sins, but that's how seriously He views the matter. Sin requires death as a payment. God, although willing to pay the payment, cannot die. Therefore, the one who saves us must be human in order to die. However, the death of an ordinary man could not pay for sin eternally. So the Savior must also be God—the God-man. And that's what we have in Jesus Christ. "Therefore, He [Christ] had to be made like His brethren [us] in all things, that He might become a merciful and faithful high priest in things pertaining to God, to make propitiation for the sins of the people" (Hebrews 2:17). It is worth pointing out again that He was like us in all things except for sin.

God is calling out people for His own possession. But He only wants people to be His who want to be His. Therefore, He allows people to choose Him. Our sins stood in the way of that. Jesus Christ, God the Son, made propitiation for our sins, making forgiveness possible. Now our sins need no longer be an obstacle to us.

This is love that is more than theoretical. This is love that gives. "For God so loved the world, that *He gave* His only begotten Son, that whoever believes in Him should not perish, but have eternal life" (John 3:16, emphasis added). This is the grace (the unmerited favor) of God; something I didn't deserve, but that God gave to me as a gift. Really, though, it's favor against merit because my sins merit judgment—eternal death in the lake of fire. "But God, being rich in mercy, because of His great love with which He loved us, even when we were dead in our transgressions, made us alive together with Christ (by grace you have been saved), and raised us up with Him, and seated us with Him in the heavenly places, in Christ Jesus, in order that in the ages to come He might show the surpassing riches of His grace in kindness toward us in Christ Jesus" (Ephesians 2:4-7).

And here, in Ephesians 2:7, we have the reason why— God's overarching purpose for creating man: "in order that in the ages to come He might show the surpassing riches of His grace in kindness toward us in Christ Jesus." As stated earlier, "This whole thing is about love."

However, the second death, the lake of fire, is still the default—what you get if you don't do something. Grace, as wonderful as it is, only makes a real choice possible. You still have to make the choice for yourself. God *allows* people to choose Him, He doesn't force them.

Understanding the Call

It is important to say again that God is just. "The Lord is righteous...He will do no injustice. Every morning He brings His justice to light; He does not fail..." (Zephaniah 3:5). Justice, like the rest of God's attributes dealing with man, must not only be, but must be seen to be. In other words, God does not have some secret form of justice that man knows nothing about. We, as created beings, have a concept of justice because we are made in the image of God. So the kind of justice we understand is God's kind of justice. This is the basis for the so-called natural law.

The reason why this is important is because God "...has fixed a day in which He will judge the world in righteousness..." (Acts 17:31). This means that each person will stand before God and give an account of himself or herself related to Christ's atoning sacrifice. Therefore God, in justice (not to mention love, mercy, and grace), will place a call upon your life. This call is an invitation to choose Him, i.e., to believe 1.) That the testimony the Bible gives regarding who Jesus is and what He has done is true, and 2.) That you realize He did it for you, for the forgiveness of your sins, and you receive it from Him as full payment for your sins forever. "O taste and see that the Lord is good; how blessed is the man [woman, boy, or girl] who takes refuge in Him!" (Psalm 34:8).

Some people may disagree with the last paragraph, but it seems to me that if God did not do this someone could conceivably stand before Him and be sent to the lake of fire claiming, correctly, that he or she never knew there was another option. That is not going to happen because God "...will do no injustice."

There are a few places in the Bible where a call is very clear from Jesus' lips: "Come to Me, all who are weary and heavy-laden, and I will give you rest" (Matthew 11:28). "...If any man is thirsty, let him come to Me and drink. He who believes in Me, as the Scripture said, 'From his innermost being shall flow rivers of living water'" (John 7:37-38). This is what theologians term a "general call." However, there is also a specific call, and the fact of that call is most often seen looking back, i.e., from the perspective of those who have responded to the call, as in 1 Thessalonians 2:12: "...that you may walk in a manner worthy of the God who *calls* you into His own kingdom and glory" (emphasis added). I think this is because the person being called experiences the call as conviction.

Conviction, in the biblical context, is *always* a work of God the Holy Spirit exposing a person's sins to his or her conscience. The Greek word means to convict or convince, but it also carries the idea of reproof and condemnation. So biblical conviction is the Holy Spirit laying the matter of a person's sins before his or her conscience in a way that condemns; showing his or her vulnerability to God's wrath.

The Holy Spirit may speak "out of the blue" to a person's conscience. He may speak through the written word. He may use someone's spoken testimony or speak through the preached word. Being God, He is not limited in how He speaks. He may use people, but if conviction comes to a person it is because of the Holy Spirit. This is not something man could think up on his own.

Sometimes a friend or relative may avoid telling you a truth about yourself so as to spare your feelings. God will always tell you the truth, even when it hurts, because He does not you to walk into disaster. Conviction is unpleasant and it hurts, but it is God's invitation and must be regarded as such. God is loving, God is merciful, God is gracious, and God is "...not wishing for any to perish..." (2 Peter 3:9). But God *allows* us to choose Him, He doesn't force us. Therefore, you may reject His invitation. Gracious as He is, He *may* convict (invite) you again, but His justice in the matter is fully satisfied if He convicts you once. So the counsel of the Bible is: "Today if you hear His voice, do not harden your hearts" (Hebrews 4:7) because "...My Spirit shall not strive with man forever" (Genesis 6:3).

Why You Should Believe

10

Why You Should Believe

T hat Jesus Christ lived as a man on earth some 2,000 years ago is probably the best recognized fact of history, attested to by both the Bible and secular sources. Therefore, most people don't question His historical existence. Some recognize Him as a "religious figure," and some even refer to Him as the Son of God. These things are part of the common knowledge. But who is Jesus—really?

The apostle John, at the opening of his gospel, tells us:

In the beginning was the Word [Jesus], and the Word [Jesus] was with God, and the Word [Jesus] was God. He [Jesus] was in the beginning with God. All things came into being by Him [Jesus], and apart from Him [Jesus] nothing came into being that has come into being. (John 1:1-3)

In the beginning, meaning the beginning of creation, Jesus was already there. This speaks of His eternality. Then John plainly tells us that Jesus *is* the eternal God, "the Word was God." He then tells us that Jesus is the creator: "All things came into being by Him, and apart from Him nothing came into being that has come into being."

How do we know that "Word" refers to Jesus? John tells us in verse 14: "And the Word became flesh, and dwelt among us, and we beheld His glory, glory as of the only begotten from the Father, full of grace and truth." So here, in the first 14 verses of John's gospel, we have both the divinity and the humanity of Jesus—the God-man.

This is the foundational understanding of the New Testament writers, who all wrote under the inspiration of the Holy Spirit. Here's what Paul has to say in Philippians 2:5-11:

> ...Christ Jesus, who, although He existed in the form of God, did not regard equality with God a thing to be grasped, but emptied Himself, taking the form of a bond-servant, and being made in the likeness of men. And being found in appearance as a man, He humbled Himself by becoming obedient to the point of death, even death on a cross. Therefore also God highly exalted Him, and bestowed on Him the name which is above every name, that at the name of Jesus every knee should bow, of those who are in heaven, and on earth, and under the earth, and that every tongue should confess that Jesus Christ is Lord, to the glory of God the Father.

Previously we said that, "God, in love, determined that He Himself would pay the penalty [of sin] for us." This was how He did it. And make no mistake; it was the work of God and not of man, for He says in Isaiah 53:6, "All of us like sheep have gone astray, each of us has turned to his own way; But the Lord [God the Father] has caused the iniquity of us all To fall on Him [God the Son]." This is the gift of God, as Paul explains in Romans 3:24-26:

> ...being **justified** as a gift by His **grace** through the **redemption** which is in **Christ Jesus**; whom God displayed publicly as a **propitiation** in **His blood** through **faith**. This was to demonstrate His righteousness, because in the **forbearance** of God He passed over the sins previously committed; for the demonstration, I say, of His righteousness at the **present time**, that He might be just and the justifier of the one who has **faith** in Jesus (emphasis added).

Let's break this down: The word **justified** is a legal term meaning "to declare righteous." God declares me righteous as a gift by His **grace** (because it is something I do not merit). He does this through **redemption** which means "the paying of a price." The word redemption here is linked to the word **propitiation** by **Christ Jesus**, God the Son, as we discussed earlier: "In this is love, not that we loved God, but that He loved us and sent His Son to be the propitiation for our sins." But here we are further told that the propitiation was in **His blood**. 1 John 1:7 tells us that "...the blood of Jesus His [God's] Son cleanses us from all sin." This is appropriated by **faith**. Faith, here, is faith in Christ Jesus as the propitiation. Blood is the price paid that satisfied God's justice; for "...without shedding of blood there is no forgiveness." (Hebrews 9:22).

The effect of this is far-reaching and is a demonstration of God's righteousness because, in His **forbearance** (choosing not to enforce the penalty), He intentionally overlooked sins previously committed. This does not mean *our* former sins. It means sins committed before the death of Christ, i.e., from Adam to Christ. God overlooked these sins with a view to the sacrifice of Christ, which was at that time still future. For example Abraham "...believed in the Lord; and He reckoned [credited] it to him as righteousness" (Genesis 15:6). Note that this *reckoning* is *always* on the basis of faith—Abraham *believed*. The immutable God has only ever had one plan to rescue sinners: by grace, through faith. And what God did for Abraham, He will do for us as a demonstration of His righteousness at the **present time** (meaning today). So our question from chapter eight— "How can God let guilty sinners into heaven and at the same time remain just?"—is answered here: That God might be just and the justifier of the one who has **faith** in Jesus. "For Christ also died for sins once for all, the just for the unjust, in order that He might bring us to God..." (1 Peter 3:18). But again notice that this is *always* on the basis of faith.

So good works—even religious good works—are excluded. We can do nothing to earn this. All we can do is receive it by faith as a gift from God's hand. "For we maintain that a man is justified by faith apart from works of the law" (Romans 3:28). And because we can do nothing to earn it boasting is also excluded. "...may it never be that I should boast, except in the cross of our Lord Jesus Christ, through which the world has been crucified to me, and I to the world" (Galatians 6:14).

The justified one is *declared* righteous, not actually made righteous in himself. The distinction is important because if I had been *made* righteous, it would be a position from which I could fall. Instead, God declares me righteous as a judicial act—a position from which I *cannot* fall. The perfect righteousness of Christ is imputed or credited to me on the basis of my sins being imputed to Christ when I believed: "He [God the Father] made Him [Christ] who knew no sin to be sin on our behalf, that we might become the righteousness of God in Him" (2 Corinthians 5:21) Any standing that the justified one has with God is *in Christ*, who bore our sins. So when God looks at me He sees the righteousness of His dear Son "...who loved me and delivered Himself up for me" (Galatians 2:20).

Two Options

Adam fell, and in him we all fell. Sickness, suffering, sorrow, fear, guilt, sin, and death has been the unhappy lot of the human race ever since. The ideal environment of the Garden of Eden couldn't prevent the entrance of sin and an ideal environment now (if one could be had) cannot cure man of the plague sin has brought upon him. But what man cannot do God *can* do and has done by His Son, the Lord Jesus Christ. This is good news for man. Paul described it very simply in 1 Corinthians 15:3-4:

> For I delivered to you as of first importance what I also received, that Christ died for our sins according to the Scriptures, and that He was buried, and that He was raised on the third day according to the Scriptures

The thing of first importance is that Christ died for our sins: "In this is love, not that we loved God, but that He loved us and sent His Son to be the propitiation for our sins." And He was well and truly dead for they buried Him. But death could not hold the sinless Son of God, who said, "...the ruler of the world...has *nothing* in Me" (John 14:30, emphasis added). And God the Father confirmed His acceptance of Christ's sacrifice, declaring Him "...the Son of God with power by the resurrection from the dead..." (Romans 1:4). Power. Power to deliver us from the bondage of sin, death, and hell. Power to "...establish [our] hearts unblamable in holiness before our God and Father..." (1 Thessalonians 3:13).

However, the default (what you get if you don't do something) is still the second death—eternal separation from God—tormented day and night, forever and ever in the lake of fire.

So, as far as eternal destiny is concerned, there are only two choices:

1. Do nothing. If everything you've read up to this point seems like nonsense to you, then do nothing. This is accepting the default, but at least you're making an informed decision.
2. Do something about it. If you've read up to this point and have the nagging feeling that what you've read is true, it might be God speaking to your heart. In that case, you'll want to read on.

Amazing Love

11

Amazing Love

What God is offering you is new life. Jesus said, "...unless one is born again, he cannot see the kingdom of God" (John 3:3). In this new life is salvation—forgiveness of sins (the acts) as well as deliverance from the power and domination of sin (the principle). He obtained this for you by His death, burial, and resurrection. Part of what this also accomplished was to render Satan powerless (with respect only to those who belong to Christ): "Since then the children [us] share in flesh and blood, He Himself [Christ] likewise also partook of the same, that through death He [Christ] might *render powerless* him who had the power of death, that is, *the devil*" (Hebrews 2:14, emphasis added). Satan no longer has power over those who belong to Christ, to dominate them—not that he won't try.

This new life is yours on one condition only—that you believe. "I am not ashamed of the gospel, for it is the power of God for salvation to everyone who *believes*" (Romans 1:16, emphasis added). And this belief is to be in Jesus Christ: "And there is salvation in no one else; for there is no other name under heaven that has been given among men, by which we must be saved" (Acts 4:12).

Someone familiar with the Bible might ask if repentance is a necessary element in receiving this new life. The answer is yes and no. Repentance, as the word is used in

85

the Bible, is a change of mind that results in a change in life direction of the one repenting. This is a vital element in saving faith, but it is comprehended in believing. If you didn't believe before, but do believe now, you've made that change. So repentance is necessary, but not as a separate act from believing.

What about faith? Faith is, of course, necessary, but faith and belief may be regarded as synonymous terms. Saving faith, when exercised, is in conjunction with conviction and has three elements: knowledge, assent, and trust. Knowledge is the knowledge of your condition: spiritually dead (empty of God) and that you have amassed sins by your lawless deeds and mark missing. Assent is your agreement with God that this knowledge is true. Trust is placing your full confidence in Jesus Christ alone as being both able and willing to forgive your sins and grant you new life. To *believe* this is to exercise faith. "But to the one who does not work, but *believes* in Him who justifies the ungodly, his *faith* is reckoned as righteousness" (Romans 4:5, emphasis added).

What to believe

In the end there is no middle ground—either you are a believer or you're not—and you would know, for, "The Spirit Himself bears witness with our spirit that we are children of God" (Romans 8:16). If you don't have that witness in yourself you have never truly believed, you are spiritually dead (empty of God), and "...dead in your trespasses and sins." (Ephesians 2:1). Your default end is the lake of fire. You don't have to go there. "...I have set before you life and death, the blessing and the curse. So choose life..." (Deuteronomy 30:19).

Christ died for your sins. Believe it. Receive it as God's gift to you, by His grace, for the full payment of your sins forever. That's all there is to it. You can formalize by saying a prayer, and you should. But it is the faith behind the prayer that appropriates. You might pray something like the following:

Dear heavenly Father. I know that I am a sinner and that there is nothing in me that would commend me to You. But I believe Your word that You love me and sent Your Son Jesus to suffer and die in my place so that I can be forgiven. I believe with all my heart that His shed blood is sufficient to cleanse me from *all* my sins; past, present, and future. I pray for that forgiveness right now and, by Your word receive Jesus Christ as my Savior, my Lord, and my Life. Thank you, Father, for loving me so much. I pray this in the wonderful name of my Savior and Lord, Jesus Christ. Amen.

The effect of what you have just done can be seen by juxtaposing man's problem with God's grace. As stated previously, man has two problems: on the one hand he is spiritually dead (empty of God), on the other he has sinned. In order for God to recognize man as fit to be in His presence, He must "see" the Holy Spirit in the man. However, the Holy Spirit will not enter man because of sin—He will not live in a house which is unclean.

Here is the great miracle of God's grace: Forgiveness of sins cleanses you: "...the blood of Jesus His Son cleanses us from all sin" (1 John 1:7). All sin means *all* sin; past, present, and future. Your "house" is clean, removing the obstacle which kept the Holy Spirit out. So the Holy Spirit moves in. This is known as the "new birth" and is what it means to be "born again." In the spiritual sense, you have been raised from the dead. What Adam lost, you have regained: "...He saved us, through the washing of regeneration and *renewal* of the Holy Spirit" (Titus 3:5 literal, emphasis added). And because *all* sin is forgiven, there is no basis upon which the Holy Spirit will ever move out: "...for He Himself has said, 'I will never desert you, nor will I ever forsake you.'" (Hebrews 13:5). The Lord Jesus Christ has given you eternal life and you are completely secure in Him forever! "My sheep hear My voice, and I know them, and they follow Me; and I give eternal life to them, and they shall never perish; and no one shall snatch them out of My hand" (John 10:27-28).

Long my imprisoned spirit lay,
Fast bound in sin and nature's night,
Thine eye diffused a quick'ning ray:
I woke—the dungeon flamed with light!
My chains fell off! My heart was free!
I rose, went forth, and followed Thee.
Amazing love! How can it be?
That Thou, my God, shouldst die for me!

—Charles Wesley

You did nothing to earn your salvation and keeping it does not depend on your ability to live a righteous life, but on Christ's omnipotent power to keep you in His hand. However, God expects you to live a righteous life: "...He died for all, that they who live should no longer live for themselves, but for Him who died and rose again on their behalf" (2 Corinthians 5:15).

Don't worry! You will want to do this and God will help you as you submit to the leading of the Holy Spirit, who now lives in you if you have believed.

Now What do I Do?

12

Now What do I Do?

One of the things I've always appreciated about the apostle Paul is his closeness to and his love for the Lord Jesus. In Galatians 1, he relates that after he came to faith in Christ he went away to Arabia for a time. Most commentators I've read believe he did this to spend time with the Lord—whether in person (as a miraculous event) or through the written Word of God is unstated, but there is a lesson in this for us.

If you have truly believed, your life will never be the same as it was before. This is because the Lord Jesus lives in you now, in the person of the Holy Spirit. "Therefore if any man [person] is in Christ, he is a new creature; the old things passed away; behold, new things have come" (2 Corinthians 5:17). Get to know Him. The best way to do this is to spend time with Him by spending time in His word—the Bible. Start with the book of John in the New Testament. This will give you a good grounding in your faith (cf. 2 Timothy 2:15). If you don't have a Bible, you can download a free copy of the Gospel of John at http://www.andyvl.com/John/john.htm. However, you should get a Bible of your own. I recommend that you start with an easy-to-read version such as the *New Living Translation* (NLT). This is a thought-to-thought translation in contemporary English. Later, as you become familiar with the concepts and doctrines of the Bible, you should move on to a good word-for-word translation like the *New American Standard Bible* or the *New King James Version*. The classic word-for-word translation is the (old) King James Version (also known as the Authorized Version or AV). This is still an excellent Bible, but it retains the old Elizabethan grammar of the 17th century. A third category of Bibles is the paraphrased versions, such as *The Message*. I recommend that you stay away from these.

Another help is a good study guide. Many people have benefitted from *Through the Bible in One Year* by Dr. Alan Stringfellow. This is a large-format paperback published by Whitaker House (ISBN 978-1-6291105-4-7). Following the studies in this book will give you an excellent "big picture" view of the entire Bible.

I have no financial interest in any of these products. I recommend them simply because I think they may be beneficial in helping you to grow in your faith.

Start attending church. Of course there are lots of churches out there, some good and some not so good. In general, look for a church where the Bible is held to be God's inerrant (free from error) Word; a church where God's Word is preached, believed, and obeyed; where God is worshipped and Christ is honored as Lord. This will put you in fellowship with other like-minded believers and will be an invaluable support to your new faith (cf. Hebrews 10:24-25).

Worship is very important, but worship is always about God and never about you. The etiology of the word *worship* is "worth + ship" (meaning to declare the worth). "For the Lord Most High is to be feared [revered], a great King over all the earth" (Psalm 47:2). Therefore, it is very important that you not offer to God in worship something that is worldly (I'll let you decide what that means), but something that truly and reverently expresses your love and gratitude for His worth—who He is and what He has done.

Pray. Get into the habit of praying. Keep the lines of communication open between you and God. Not only does He love you but He has time for you and you can go to Him with anything (cf. 1 Thessalonians 5:16-18). If you commit a sin, go to Him immediately in prayer and confess it. "If we confess our sins, He is faithful and righteous to forgive us our sins and to cleanse us from all unrighteousness" (1 John 1:9).

Live the life. The Christian life is not difficult to live—it is impossible. This is something that only the Lord Jesus can do *through* you. The key to living the Christian life lies in understanding that when He redeemed you it was not strictly to get you out of hell and into heaven—although that is true and gloriously so. It was to get Christ out of heaven and into you so that you can be His eyes to see with, His ears to hear with, His heart to love with, His mouth to speak with, His feet to go with, and His hands with which to work.

You will see in many places in the book of John how He perfectly demonstrated this life in His relationship to the Father. "...as the Father gave Me commandment, even so I do..." (John 14:31). Also see: John 7:16-17, 8:28-29, 12:44-50, and 14:10-11.

This is the relationship the Lord Jesus is waiting to live through you. "...as the Father has sent Me, I also send you" (John 20:21).

However, it is not something you can do in your own power, but by faith and only by faith. Success and joy in the Christian life is in the measure of your availability to Him to live His life through you, and is accomplished by:

> ➢ Your love *for* God, reciprocating His love for you and evidenced by
> ➢ Your dependence *on* God. This is expressed by
> ➢ Your obedience *to* God.

Through this you will find renewed in your person the relationship with God that Adam lost. It won't happen overnight, but will be more and more the truth of your life as you "...press on toward the goal for the prize of the upward call of God in Christ Jesus" (Philippians 3:14). May God bless you as you seek to live for Christ and let Him live through you.

Finally, tell others. You have received the greatest of all possible gifts. Perhaps your friends and relatives also desire this gift of eternal life and the grace that you have found in our wonderful Lord Jesus Christ.

To Him be the glory, both now and to the day of eternity. Amen.

Andy Van Loenen loves to hear from readers and can be contacted via his web site, www.andyvl.com.

13731664R00059